SAVING OUR PLANET

CONSERVE IT!

Mary Boone

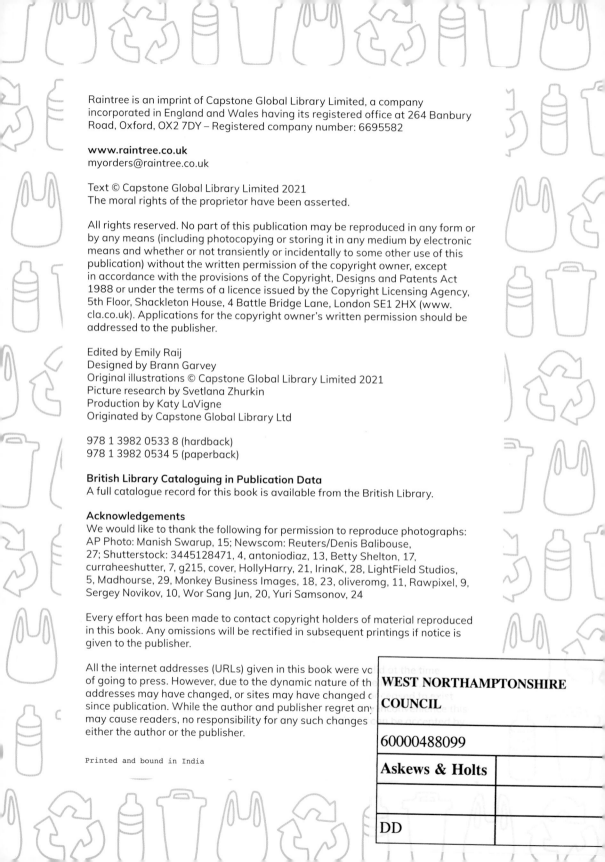

Raintree is an imprint of Capstone Global Library Limited, a company incorporated in England and Wales having its registered office at 264 Banbury Road, Oxford, OX2 7DY – Registered company number: 6695582

www.raintree.co.uk
myorders@raintree.co.uk

Edited by Emily Raij
Designed by Brann Garvey
Original illustrations © Capstone Global Library Limited 2021
Picture research by Svetlana Zhurkin
Production by Katy LaVigne
Originated by Capstone Global Library Ltd

978 1 3982 0533 8 (hardback)
978 1 3982 0534 5 (paperback)

British Library Cataloguing in Publication Data
A full catalogue record for this book is available from the British Library.

Acknowledgements
We would like to thank the following for permission to reproduce photographs: AP Photo: Manish Swarup, 15; Newscom: Reuters/Denis Balibouse, 27; Shutterstock: 3445128471, 4, antoniodiaz, 13, Betty Shelton, 17, curraheeshutter, 7, g215, cover, HollyHarry, 21, IrinaK, 28, LightField Studios, 5, Madhourse, 29, Monkey Business Images, 18, 23, oliveromg, 11, Rawpixel, 9, Sergey Novikov, 10, Wor Sang Jun, 20, Yuri Samsonov, 24

Every effort has been made to contact copyright holders of material reproduced in this book. Any omissions will be rectified in subsequent printings if notice is given to the publisher.

Printed and bound in India

CONTENTS

Words in **bold** are in the glossary.

WATER AND ENERGY

You brush your teeth. You have a shower. You eat food cooked in an oven. You turn on lights in your bedroom. You use water and **energy** every day.

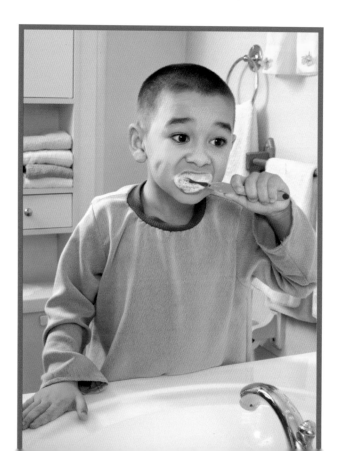

Water and energy make life easy and fun. But their supplies are limited. In order to save our planet, we must learn to **conserve**, or save, it. Work to help save the planet is called conservation.

Cars, aeroplanes and **factories** use energy. So do things that plug in or use batteries. People use a lot of energy. The number of people in the world is growing. Soon, more people will use even more energy.

Some energy is made using oil or coal. Burning oil and coal makes smoke. Smoke can **pollute** the air. Breathing the dirty air is bad for your health. **Drilling** is needed to get oil and coal out of the ground. That can harm the places where animals and people live.

An oil drilling platform

CONSERVING ENERGY

Conserving energy does not mean using no energy. It means using less. If everyone used less energy, we would need less oil and coal. Our air would be cleaner. We would have more clean water for everybody to use.

Conserving energy is easy. Adults can do it. Children can do it. You can do it at home and at school. Even small changes can make a big difference.

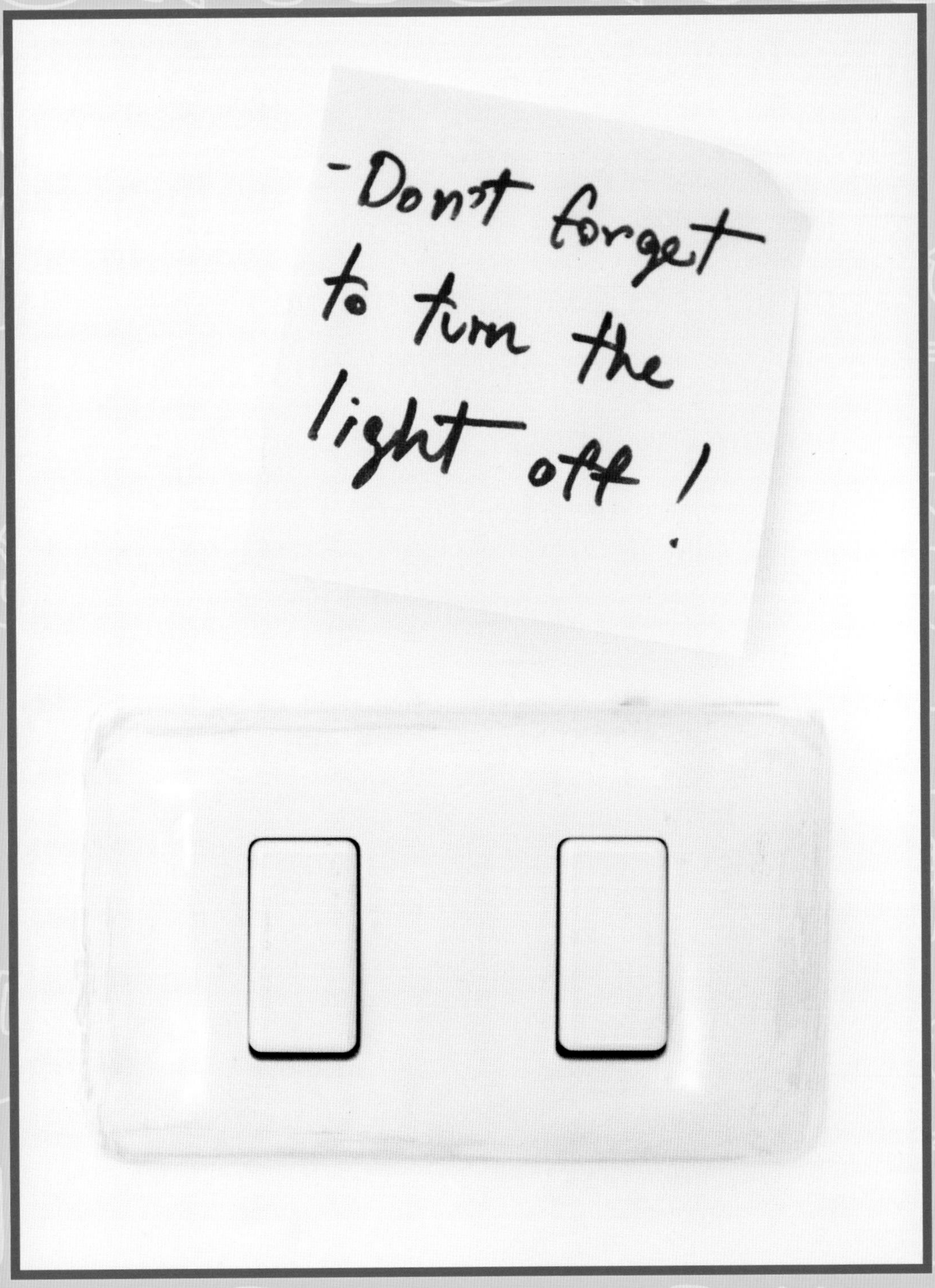
-Don't forget to turn the light off!

Try to save energy at home. Watch less TV. Play fewer video games. Turn off lights or switches when you leave a room. Do more activities that don't use energy. These could be reading, making some art or playing outside.

Think about how you and your family travel. Try walking to school. Share a lift with a friend to sports clubs. Catch the bus when you can. Fewer cars on the road means less energy being used.

Help your family conserve energy. Look around your house for ways to save energy. Can you wear a jumper instead of turning up the heating? Does everyone turn off the light when they leave the room? Can you make a meal without using **electricity**?

Test yourselves. Give a prize to the family member who does the best job of turning off lights.

Ridhima Pandey lives in India. She was five years old when she learned about pollution and how it harms the world. She started saving energy to help. She taught her friends how to as well.

At the age of nine, Ridhima met with her country's leaders. She asked them to make laws about conserving energy. She told them saving energy helps the planet. She is standing up for her beliefs. Ridhima Pandey is a conservation **activist**.

SAVING WATER

Energy is not the only thing you should save. Water is limited. Just 1 per cent of Earth's water can be used by people. The rest is saltwater or is frozen.

Plants, animals and people need to drink water. Without water, your body stops working. People can only live a few days without it.

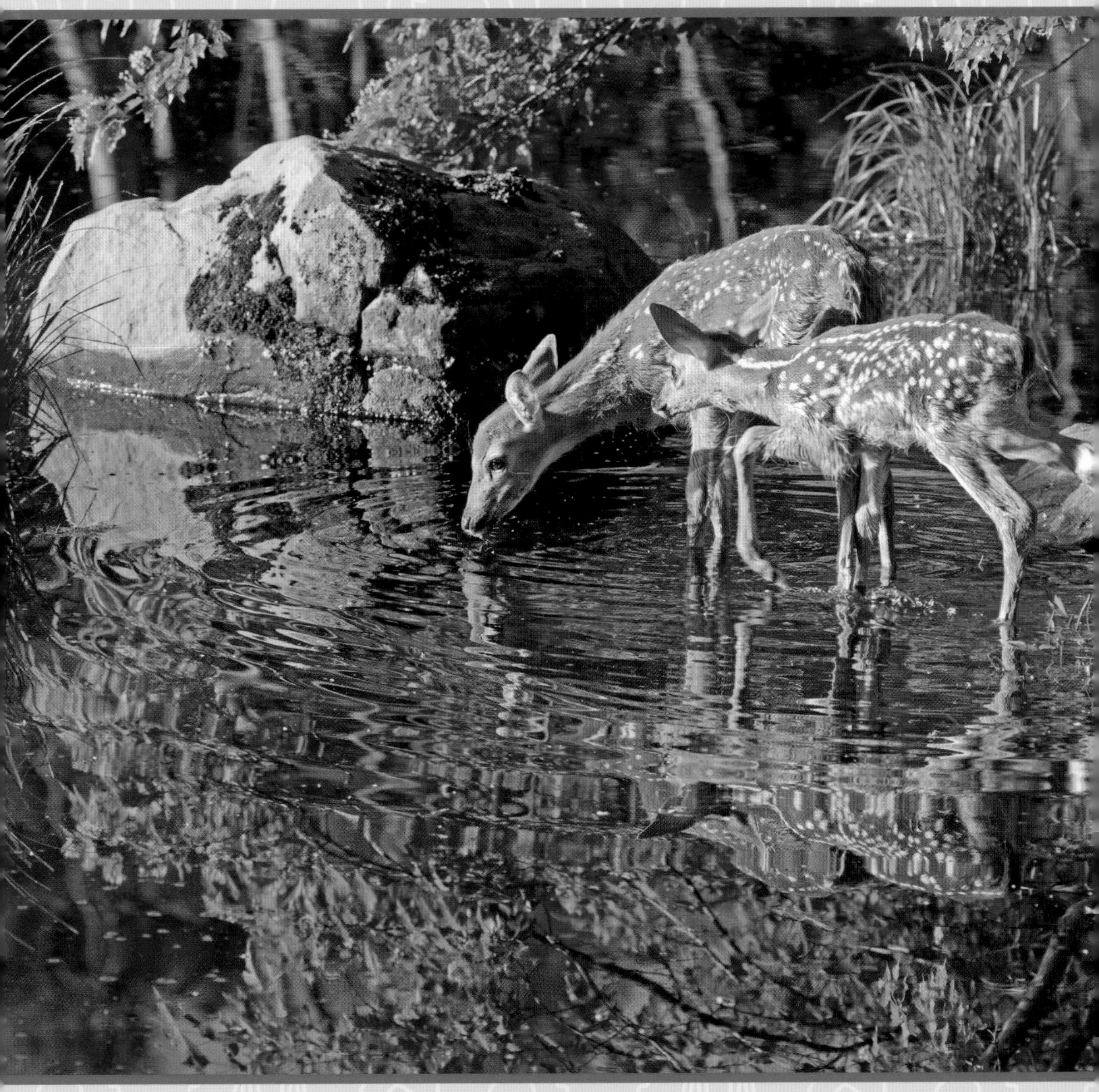

People use water for drinking and cooking. We also use it for washing and cleaning. Each person in the UK uses about 142 litres (37.5 gallons) of water each day.

Cities use water to fight fires and clean streets. Businesses and factories use water too. Restaurants need water to cook and wash dishes. Farms use lots of water to grow food. Water is even used to make electricity.

Remember, saving energy means not using more than you need. You should still brush your teeth. You should wash your face and hands. But you can save water by turning off the tap while you brush or rub.

A bath takes twice as much water as a shower. Short showers take less water than long showers. You should aim to have a shower for five minutes or less. Each minute cut from your shower saves 7.5 litres (1.6 gallons) of water.

Need more ideas for saving water?
Wash your family's car with a bucket
and sponge instead of a hose. Collect
rainwater for your garden. Dry yourself
off using the same towel for several
days. Less laundry uses less water.
Sweep your driveway instead of
spraying it with a hose.

When you give your pet fresh water,
don't pour the old water down the sink.
Use it to water plants.

Get your family to save energy too. Help your parents check for leaky taps. One drip each second adds up to 19 litres (4.2 gallons) per day. That's a lot of wasted water!

Keep a full jug of water in the fridge. Then you won't need to run the tap for so long to get cold water. Ask about switching to a shower head that saves water. That will save energy needed to heat the extra water too.

Autumn Peltier is part of Canada's Wiikwemkoong First Nation. She grew up near Lake Huron. She and her family had clean water. She knows others are not so lucky. Many places have unsafe drinking water.

Autumn began helping to solve this problem when she was eight years old. Now, she is a teenager. She is still fighting for clean drinking water for all. Saving water helps make sure more people get clean water.

Earth is our home. People can harm it. But people can also clean it up and care for it. Learning to conserve energy helps the **environment**.

Look for ways you can save energy and water. Turn the light switches off. Turn off the taps. What other ways can you help?

GLOSSARY

activist person who works for social or political change

conserve save and use in a way that stops something from being wasted or lost

drill make a hole

electricity natural force that can be used to make light and heat or to make machines work

energy usable power that comes from sources such as electricity or heat

environment all of the trees, plants, water and soil

factory building where workers make goods

pollute make dirty or unsafe

FIND OUT MORE

BOOKS

Go Green!: Join the Green Team and Learn How to Reduce, Reuse and Recycle, Liz Gogerly (Franklin Watts, 2018)

Greta Thunberg and the Climate Crisis, Amy Chapman (Franklin Watts, 2020)

What A Waste: Rubbish, Recycling and Protecting our Planet, Jess French (DK Children, 2019)

WEBSITES

climatekids.nasa.gov/menu/big-questions/
Read about climate change on the NASA website.

www.bbc.co.uk/bitesize/topics/zp22pv4/articles/z2md82p
Find out more about how humans affect the environment at BBC Bitesize.

www.natgeokids.com/uk/discover/science/nature/conservation-tips/
This website has lots of tips on how you can help save the planet.

INDEX